MW00618840

Powerful Leadership Skills for Women

Written by Dr. Patricia Murdock Miller
Edited by National Press Publications

NATIONAL PRESS PUBLICATIONS

A Division of Rockhurst College Continuing Education Center, Inc.

6901 West 63rd Street • P.O. Box 2949 • Shawnee Mission, Kansas 66201-1349

1-800-258-7246 • 1-913-432-7757

Table of Contents

1

WHERE ARE YOU NOW?

"Old tapes" of who we were may no longer be appropriate today. Should you take time to look for your blocking behaviors? If you're like most of us, you have an Achilles' Heel or Albatross you just can't shake. Here's how to stop playing those "old tapes" once and for all:

Four Steps to Re-programming for Success

1. Recognize your blocking behaviors.
2. Throw them away.
3. Give yourself permission to change.
4. Re-program yourself.

Recognition

The first key to change is **recognizing** your blocking behaviors. Many quizzes have been devised to help managers look inside themselves for barriers to effectiveness. Can you recognize some parts of your behaviors in the following Self-Exploration Checklist? Use this as an opportunity to explore and seek out your tendencies—you may find some useless baggage!

Self-Exploration Checklist

*Check the questions that ring somewhat true with you. Do it
quickly without making deep judgments.*

_____ 1. Do you have trouble assigning important projects to subordinates?

_____ 2. Do you think your subordinate won't complete an assignment as well as you would?

_____ 3. Do you have trouble asking for assistance?

_____ 4. Are you reluctant to offer suggestions because you fear rejection?

_____ 5. Do you have trouble accepting criticism from your boss?

_____ 6. Do you prefer a "rule to follow" approach when doing your job?

_____ 7. Do you prefer the routine part of your job as opposed to the unexpected parts?

_____ 8. Do you have trouble adapting to a change at work?

_____ 9. Do you over-supervise as opposed to under-supervise your subordinates?

_____10. Do you lose sight of what you're trying to accomplish because you're working so hard to do it?

_____11. Do you become overextended at work?

_____12. Do you make promises or commitments at work that you can't meet?

_____13. Do you have trouble saying "no"?

_____14. Do you put off dealing with problem subordinates?

_____15. Do you have trouble telling your subordinates that their work wasn't acceptable?

_____16. Do you feel excessive stress at work?

_____17. Do you explode in anger and don't quite know why?

_____18. Do your subordinates sometimes misunderstand your directions, expectations and requests?

_____19. When you make unpopular decisions, do you prefer telling your subordinates that it's mostly due to the departmental policies or your boss's orders?

_____20. Do you find yourself needing your subordinates to like you?

_____21. Do you prefer the *technical* or doing part of your job over the *managing* and coordinating part?

_____22. Do you understand how your department functions but not how the total company competes with its competitors?

_____23. Do you prefer planning from day to day over laying out what needs to be accomplished next month?

_____24. Is your vision of what will happen at work vague?

____25. Do you find a lot of your time at work is spent trying to smooth out unexpected problems?

____26. Do you have to tell your subordinates what to do next?

____27. Do you have trouble visualizing your next job position?

____28. Do you see your work as a job versus a career?

____29. Do you often wait for your boss to give you directions?

____30. Are you reluctant to go ahead with an idea until you have approval?

____31. Do you prefer to keep out of arguments even when you might have something to say?

____32. Do you see conflict as negative?

____33. Do you dislike "tooting your horn" to your boss when you accomplish a tough project?

____34. Do you dislike high visibility?

____35. Do you dislike playing politics at work?

____36. Does the word "power" mean something negative?

____37. Is relating to males at work uncomfortable?

____38. Does supervising a male create images of a problem situation?

____39. Do you feel discounted as a manager when you participate in groups of males at meetings or informally?

____40. Do you feel like you don't know what to do to advance "up the ladder" in your organization?

Directions for Scoring:

Items 1-10: If 3 or more are checked you may have "Being Perfect" problems.

Items 11-20: If 3 or more are checked you may have the "Pleasing Others" habit.

Items 21-22: Are you not letting go of your "Specialist/Detail" perspective?

Items 23-24: Are you focusing on the short term?

Items 25-26: Are you a "Reactor"?

Items 27-28: Do you want a *job* or a *career*?

Items 29-30: Are you a follower?

Items 31-32: Can you conceive of conflict as positive?

Items 33-34: Are you taking a low profile?

Items 35-36: Can you see power and politics positively?

Items 37-38: Are males a problem?

Item 39: Are you discounted?

Item 40: Can you map where to go from here?

Carefully read the sections you checked. You may recognize some of your barriers.

"Being Perfect" Scenario: Items 1-10

Marlene, department manager of quality control, is a high achiever and a hard worker. Everyone says, "Give her the project if you want it done right." That's why she got promoted. She disliked substandard performance. She gives her subordinates small, insignificant tasks and jobs and checks everything they do. She does most of the important projects. There is only one way to do things—her way. Marlene never circumvents the rules or formal channels; if there isn't a standard procedure to follow, she gets uneasy. Marlene is reluctant to offer suggestions at staff meetings and dislikes any discussions about changing procedures. When a new computer system was installed, it caused her much stress, anger and resentment. The computer support staff wondered why she never asked for assistance and insisted on doing it on her own—mostly learning the new system at night. When her supervisor suggested she call Computer Support for a short training program for her department, Marlene "blew up" and walked out in anger. She knew that her department's efficiency and productivity were low, but she was already working at top capacity.

What's happening with Marlene? Do you recognize the following tendencies or blocking characteristics?

Blocking Characteristics of "Being Perfect"

1. Doing everything results in stress and low productivity.
2. Not asking for help results in inefficiency.
3. Difficulty adapting to change results in little progress.
4. Excessive use of rules and the formal organization means doing it the hard way.
5. Fear of being wrong means you're seen as lacking initiative.
6. Not delegating means you're not developing your employees.
7. Over-supervising results in low subordinate morale.
8. One way—your way—results in low subordinate morale.
9. Uneasiness with uncertain conditions results in lost time and lost opportunities.
10. Resisting criticism results in never improving or developing your management potential.

Four Steps to Solving the "Being Perfect" Problem

Step 1   Recognize you're trading personal approval and rewards for effectiveness in your department. Recognize that managing is not doing it yourself but *getting it done through others*. You're being evaluated on what you can get your subordinates to do. Your department's work performance will increase when you let go of the *"doer"* role and assume the *manager* role.

Step 2 Throw away any blocking characteristics of being perfect that are cheating you, your subordinates and your department of success.

Step 3 Give yourself permission to be less than perfect: to risk being wrong, to develop your management skills (you already have the technical and doing skills), to develop your employees, and to listen to criticism and hear the feedback on what needs to change.

Step 4 Re-program yourself. Assume the behaviors and traits of successful people. Learn the tasks and people skills of management.

"Pleasing Everyone" Scenario: Items 11-20

Patricia, manager of the Training department, is tense and overloaded most of the time. When asked if she could start a new program with the Marketing department, she committed to it. At times she feels reluctant to ask her staff to do unpleasant training programs such as this new one she promised. Also, one of her subordinates causes her a lot of headaches. She keeps telling herself that she'll talk to the problem subordinate about being late with proposals. What she really finds problematic is the tendency her staff has of seeming to not know what she means when she talks about quality. When she alludes to improving the training programs, they should know what she is really talking about. She hates being direct because her staff might be offended. At the end of the day she asks herself why she took on a new program with a deadline she knew she could not meet. Besides, her staff might get flippant and cold with her again. Walking to her car she asks herself, "Why do I get wrapped up in trying to get them to like me?"

What's happening with Patricia? Do you recognize some typical blocking characteristics?

Blocking Characteristics of "Pleasing Everyone"

1. Over-committing, not being able to say "no" results in stress and broken promises.

2. Avoiding confronting subordinate problems results in further
   deterioration of performance.
3. Not being direct because it's too offensive results in misunder-
   standings, missed directions and performance deterioration.
4. Wanting to be liked can be excessive when the result is avoidance
   of giving direction, feedback and guidance. You're cheating
   everyone when ''not offending'' takes precedence over being an
   effective manager.

Four Steps to Solving ''Pleasing Everyone''

1. Recognize you're trading ''being liked'' for effectiveness, efficiency
   and performance.
2. Stop: a) making promises you can't keep.
          b) not being able to say ''no.''
          c) avoiding confrontation of problem subordinates.
          d) indirect communication.
          e) putting wanting to ''be liked'' above all else.
3. Give yourself permission to change this ineffective barrier to
   success.
4. Re-program yourself. People like and respect you when you're
   honest about constraints on your time. Subordinates will like and
   respect you in the long run if you assist them in correcting their
   problems. Honest, direct communication is never offensive in the
   long run because everyone profits when expectations are clearly
   communicated.

''Specialist and Detail'' Scenario: Items 21-22

This is a natural result of being promoted out of the ''doer''
job to the manager job. Recognition that you need to broaden your
perspective to see the ''big picture'' helps resolve this one.

''Short Term'' Scenario: Items 23-24

Begin to think in the long term as well as the short term. What
do you, your subordinates and your department need to plan for
next month, in six months, in one year or longer?

''Reactor'' Scenario: Items 25-26

Acquire the task of management called planning. There are
many benefits to a plan. Subordinates know what to do, how to do it
and what criteria of success is expected. You and your department
will be more effective.

"Job or Career" Scenario: Items 27-28

Do you have a career path laid out? Where do you want to go in the future? If you don't have a career path laid out, then perhaps you want a job, not a career.

"Follower" Scenario: Items 29-30

Managing and supervising require a leader orientation. Initiative behavior is a requirement for success. Leaders have the skills of directing, guiding, planning and controlling for effectiveness.

"Positive Conflict" Scenario: Items 31-32

If you can only see the downside of conflict, you'll be hindered in your problem-solving skill development. Conflict gets the real issues "out on the table" so the problem can be resolved.

"Low Profile" Scenario: Items 33-34

A low profile might be safe, but it locks you out of being seen as a "go-getter." You'll miss a lot of opportunities to show what you can do. You might even miss a promotion.

"Positive Power and Politics" Scenario: Items 35-36

Power is personal influence, and is needed for effectiveness and advancement. Politics can appear negative, but when you understand it establishes reciprocal obligations between yourself and others to help each other in times of need, it is a positive act.

"Male Problem" Scenario: Items 37-38

Sexual harassment still occurs, but knowing how to confront it increases your confidence. Supervising males can become, with practice, just like supervising anyone. Supervision can be a non-gender issue.

"Being Discounted" Scenario: Item 39

It happens to many of us. Knowing what to do to establish credibility can eliminate this discounting.

"Where to Go From Here?" Scenario: Item 40

Charting out a career map is critical if you want to advance. Knowing how to do this enhances your development.

Permission to Manage and Re-program for Success

We all carry enough around without also carrying useless baggage such as attitudes of "trying for perfection." Aaron Miller, a wise philosopher, said, "No one's perfect and no one can make it without help." When pleasing others becomes a problem, you are—in actuality—pleasing no one; not you, not your subordinates and not your organization. If you identified some of your barriers, you've started down the road to effective management. Re-program yourself by carefully reading the chapters in this handbook.

Good Luck and Good Managing!

2

BEHAVIORS AND TRAITS OF ALL SUCCESSFUL PEOPLE

Leaders Are Made, Not Born

Management, leadership and supervisory skills are acquired by those who want to manage. No one is born with the ability to step into management.

Susan, recently promoted to management from her position of administrative assistant, was delighted to learn that she possessed the necessary characteristics and behaviors to make the switch from "doer" to manager. She had worked hard, met deadlines, planned her boss's work week and exhibited initiative. She knows who to ask to get a job done, how to get cooperation, how to handle difficult people and how her boss's job fit into other departmental plans. Susan spent her time in the administrative assistant job as on-the-job training for management. She was an astute observer and quickly learned many behaviors and traits of successful managers. In her words, "I'm ready to tackle the rest of my training." She is indeed ready.

What are the behaviors and traits of successful people? Let's examine the most significant behaviors and traits.

Traits of Successful People

1. *Initiative:* It's 3 p.m. and your boss is gone. A phone call *and* a crisis have just occurred. A plant in the western part of the state needs a rush order by tomorrow morning. You can't reach your boss. You don't have the authority to order UPS delivery. What would you do? Call shipping or manufacturing, let them authorize it, and you finish the job.
2. *Flexibility:* You follow a particular procedure for authorizations of credit. You're familiar with this method and can crank out one a minute if necessary. A subordinate has devised a faster, more efficient method that also electronically records the transaction. You know takes you and everyone else longer to complete the authorizations using the new procedure. However, the subordinate points out that it accomplishes two procedures—authorization and record-keeping. Also, after you're familiar with it, it will go faster. Can you adapt to this change? Can you authorize it on its merits and not your preferences?
3. *Self-Control, Self-Direction, Self-Knowledge:* Carole, supervisor of the R & D department, sat on her angry feelings when she found herself staying late to complete a large research project for the department's long-term needs. The next morning she jumped down the throats of two of her subordinates because they were two minutes late. Another supervisor asked her what was wrong. Carole explained, "I was fed up with their irresponsibility; I worked until 8 last night and I got here on time." The other supervisor asked, "Why were you here and they weren't?" The story unfolded that Carole did not want to bother them because they were still tender about her promotion and they might get angry. Do you recognize that Carole seems to be more concerned about whether they like her than whether the job gets done? She is also reluctant to delegate large jobs and develop her subordinates. Carole doesn't have a clear sense of who she is or what motivates her. Control over her environment and self seems to be lacking. Don't trade being liked for departmental effectiveness. Don't cheat your subordinates out of developmental guidance because of your own needs. Know why you're angry; Carole was probably angry at herself for not delegating part of the project and telling them to stay and work. She needs to scratch below the surface of her behavior and recognize her own barriers to effectiveness.
4. *Efficiency-Oriented:* Carole's problem also illustrates a lack of efficiency orientation. Why should a salaried management person be working late when another alternative is clearly available?

Delegating would have been more cost-efficient and would have freed her to do more managerial planning so a late night rush could be avoided.

5. *Communication—Clear, Direct and Concise:* How could Carole have demonstrated a clear, direct and concise message to her subordinates? First, she could have talked with her group about her promotion as soon as it occurred and explained her new role and need for teamwork. Second, when the large R & D project was assigned she should have broken it into parts, assessed her subordinates' strengths and weaknesses and delegated it. Third, when the deadline occurred, the reluctance to ask them to stay wouldn't have occurred because they had already worked through the tenderness of her promotion and were part of a team on the project. A natural occurrence would be to have finished the project earlier (according to a plan Carole should have set up) or for all team members to stay late if the planning schedule was not met. The explosion wouldn't have occurred because of Carole's earlier actions: discussion, delegation and clear message of expectation.

6. *Confidence and High Self-Esteem:* Barbara was attending a relatively high-level strategic planning meeting as a new member. The discussion involved the long-range planning needs to meet the corporation's strategy. The vice president of planning, three management levels above Barbara, asked her what she thought about the strategy of adding a new product line to diversify the corporation's risk. Barbara had some knowledge of the new product line and how it would fit with the other lines; however, she didn't have any in-depth information. She didn't know anyone in the group. What would you do? Because Barbara does have a high sense of confidence and self-esteem, she offered her opinions and qualified them as opinions. She did venture some speculation on the fit between the lines and the cost-effectiveness of using the same distribution system. She behaved and spoke with confidence. This impressed the vice president. Barbara was assigned to a high level task group because she possessed the valued trait of confidence.

7. *Comfortable With Uncertainty and Ambiguity:* Many decisions made in organizations, especially as one moves up the ladder, involve situations for which you may not have enough information to make a decision. The simple link between decision and result is lacking. Barbara's assignment to the task group will involve making decisions under uncertainty. The group will research, gather data and forecast what the consumer will buy, how much and what the cost structure will be. Production, inventory and pricing decisions will be recommended. Being comfortable with such ambiguous conditions is just one valued trait of successful managers.

8. ***Conceptual, Logical and Creative Problem Solver:*** Successful managers must be able to pull together relevant and sometimes piecemeal information into a meaningful framework. They must be able to discriminate between relevant and irrelevant information. They can do this in a somewhat logical and even intuitive manner. At the same time they can bring new meaning to old data by creatively restructuring it. That one valued trait that makes the difference between an okay decision and a high-impact decision—creativity. A large consumer products firm was threatened by a boycott of the company's products. The group threatening to call a boycott had the money and support of a large segment of the population. Key executives were trying to decide if they would remove their advertising from several television shows that the boycotting group felt should not be aired. Most executives didn't want to appear to cave in to the threat. Others felt that removal of advertising dollars from these shows would not alter the ability to reach the target consumer. Sharon, a mid-level marketing executive, proposed a creative solution. She reminded the executives that the advertising agencies were also complaining that there were few choices of other, more acceptable programs. They also felt there needed to be some changes at the network level. Sharon suggested their company representatives meet with the other five larger consumer products companies and form a coalition. She further proposed including the ad agencies in the coalition. If this coalition met with the group threatening the boycott and could reach some agreement, the problems could be resolved and meet everyone's objectives. The coalition's pressure on the networks would result in better programming. It did and Sharon's skill as a logical and creative problem solver was recognized. She was fast-tracked into further development and advancement. Her ability is another valued management trait.

9. ***Assertive—Concern for Self, Others and Organizations:*** Harold is the department head of the support function of duplication and paper flow. The Communications department had a brochure that needed duplicating and distribution. They wanted it *YESTERDAY!* Harold could promise a rush job, mobilize his staff, put other projects on hold, pay overtime and get it out by tomorrow. But, the other projects are also vital. Harold explained the constraints and the necessity of other projects—he stressed cost considerations and generally tried to problem-solve the situation with the Communications department. By asserting his needs and the organization's other project needs, he was able to determine that the "rush" project could actually wait one more day. If Harold couldn't say "no," he might have promised to complete the pro-

ject. The losers would have been him, his department and the organization. Perhaps, if he promised but was unable to deliver the project, the consequences would have been ill feelings all around. Also, the Communications department would be inclined to cry "rush" more often because of fear that future projects would not be completed on schedule.

10. ***Anticipatory:*** The ability to plan for the unexpected or the low probability event is a necessary trait in management. Johnson and Johnson did not anticipate the first Tylenol scare. Still, they were able to cope effectively because of a strong internal cultural system which prioritized the consumer's welfare above all other groups. Nevertheless, the company now has a contingency plan that can be activated within minutes in case of any product defect. Union Carbide did not have contingency plans to cope with the Bhopal incident. The consequences were negative for all parties. As a manager on any level, the possibility of unusual events occurring is always something you should recognize. In your present position, have you assessed the possibilities? What are they? What plan do you have for (1) computer shutdown (2) overload work demands (3) sick personnel (4) unexpected resignations (5) rapid growth (6) your promotion (7) budget constraints due to cutbacks (8) an unqualified workforce pool?

11. ***Cooperative:*** Katherine is a manager who utilizes cooperation to her advantage, her colleagues' and organization's. Many joint projects between groups in her department have relied on her ability to gain the support, cooperation and shared resources of others. When her agency announced a new service to the public, the need to have the personnel trained, support materials available and the proper level of scheduled employees on that day required a cooperative effort.

12. ***Can Use Personal Influence, Power:*** Margaret probably wouldn't use the word "power" to explain her behavior, but she certainly knows how to use power. Power is nothing more than the ability to influence. Margaret can access and retrieve information and data from the management information system of the organization. She has expert information power. Others know that she can do things with the system that no one else can. Margaret shares this power and influences others for the achievement of organizational and departmental goals. Others do favors for Margaret's department in exchange. Due to this reciprocity, Margaret's departmental goals are easily met and others' goals are, too.

13. ***Use of Informal Organization:*** The example of Margaret also

shows us what can be accomplished when the reciprocity involves the use of informal network of an organization.

14. ***Positive Attitude:*** Patricia's department had to process 50 percent more applications one week and send authorizations by Friday. Three of her 10 employees were out sick. She's always an upbeat person—her attitude is, "I can do it, you can do it and together we *will* do it." Her employees are infected with the same optimism. They pulled together, hired one temporary worker and accomplished the "impossible" task by the "impossible" deadline.

15. ***Good Interpersonal Social Skills:*** John had to bring together a panel of experts from three states to participate in a conference. He had no authority to order their participation and no benefits were available for the panel participants. His interpersonal skills were the only vehicle that he could call on. This situation isn't unusual in management. Can you convince others to do something?

16. ***System Knowledge:*** Do you know how your job fits into your department? Do you know how your department fits into the total organization? Is your physical organization part of a diversified corporation? Do you understand how the system of jobs, work groups, departments, functional areas and territorial groups operates? Could you state the total system's goals, strategy and plans? Are you able to translate total plans into subplans? Do you know who occupies key positions at the various levels, in various departments? Do you understand how the Marketing department, Sales department and Production department work together? If you do, then you have knowledge of your system.

17. ***Political Savvy:*** Joan quickly found out how pleading ignorance of the politics in organizations can get you in trouble. She continually put down Mr. Roberts because she saw no visible sign that he did anything productive. It wasn't a good situation—he didn't come in on time, he took very long lunches, he missed most meetings and was out of his office most of the time. Nevertheless, most people knew that he was the CEO's brother-in-law. He had founded the company and had the board appoint his wife's brother the CEO. Mr. Roberts was respected by top management. Most business from other companies was due to his presence in the corporation. Needless to say, Joan was complaining about the wrong person. Fortunately, her boss decided that she had management potential and began to explain the "do's and don'ts" of political life. Joan acquired a much needed mentor and knowledge of the political system.

18. ***Able to Give and Receive Constructive Criticism:*** This is a
    tough one for many people. For some people, though, it's a
    "walk in the park." The key to acquiring this ability is
    understanding. You can substitute the word "criticism" with
    "feedback" and it becomes a positive action. Feedback is a
    necessary part of all growth. It can come automatically through
    your job's effectiveness, but more often it comes from one's
    superior. If you can't accept feedback, you can't modify your
    behavior, efforts and performance for improvement. If you have
    trouble accepting it, you're going to try and avoid giving it.
    You're cheating your employees if you don't let them know what
    needs improvement.

*You already have many of these behaviors and traits. Acquire the
rest and you're on your way to the top!*

3

PLANNING (SETTING OBJECTIVES) AND CONTROL (KEEPING SCORE)

Planning is setting goals and objectives for the organization, division, department or the work unit. Top managers set long-range goals for the total organization such as growth levels, competitive strategies, new product development or capital investment. Middle-level managers translate long-range goals into shorter or mid-range objectives and implementation plans for the division or department such as the number of personnel or salespeople needed to accomplish a long-range plan. Supervisors further translate the mid-range goals into plans to assist in the implementation of the goal action plan. Supervisors set shorter-range plans such as new policies, work methods and work assignments, performance or efficiency objectives. All plans help meet the organizational objectives. All plans give guidance, direction and proposed time schedules. Plans at all levels must be monitored and kept on track. This is the control process.

Controlling is a natural and necessary part of planning. It's the process of "keeping score." It is comparing *actual* performance with the *planned* performance objectives. It is taking corrective action, if needed, to ensure that objectives are met.

PLANNING PROCEDURE

Planning for New Products: Example

Donna, a manager of a manufacturing plant, knows that a new cosmetic line will be added this month. The Research and Development department has sent over specifications for the production process and the Marketing department has projected the level of production to meet the new line's introduction. Donna must now pull together a plan for the plant. Decisions must be made that will affect all areas of the plant such as: new equipment, raw materials inventory, level of finished product inventory, number of employees, work assignments, scheduling and coordination with Shipping department. She calls a meeting with her subordinates. A plan of action is developed. To each subordinate group, she delegates similar activities. The subordinates are responsible for pulling their group together. Greg, a supervisor in the Cream Products Group, is delegated the responsibility of gearing up for one makeup product. He, in turn, sets a plan of action. Greg's current equipment will be able to manufacture the product. His current level of subordinates will be able to meet the increased production level. He'll need to schedule production runs, assign subordinates to certain jobs, set up time schedules and coordinate with shipping and handling. He must set standards such as number of units and quality of units. These standards will be communicated to his subordinates so they will be guided and directed with expected performance criteria. A procedure for measuring whether they're meeting the standards is established; this procedure is called *control* (or keeping score).

The term *control* sounds negative, but it is a necessary part of management. You should view it as analogous to a thermostat keeping a heating and air conditioning system performing correctly. Control aids in accomplishing desired objectives. The process is like a score card at a baseball game. It's the method or series of methods used to track the results of planning, organizing and leading. The control process helps managers adjust plans and take corrective action as needed. The steps of the control process compare measured performance against established standards, reinforcing success and correcting shortcomings.

The Three Indicators of an Effective Plan

1. *Guides People:* Tells who will do what and how.
2. *Has Measurable Results:* Tells the level and quality of performance that is expected.

3. **Provides Feedback:** Tells people if the goals are met.

Six Steps to Effective Planning

1. State *what* needs to be done (goals).
2. State *how* to get it done (action steps).
3. State *who* will do it (delegation).
4. State *when* it will be done (timetable).
5. State *standards* to know if it's accomplished (performance criteria).
6. Compare *actual results* with standards (control).

4

ORGANIZING FOR EFFECTIVENESS

"We Have to Get Organized"

This expression is routinely heard throughout any organization—volunteer groups, families, corporations and departments. A truism always acknowledged but seldom accomplished!

Organizing Under Stable Conditions

To Tom, a tomato sauce plant manager, organizing means deciding *what* the department has to accomplish, *how* it's going to do it and finding a *procedure* it can follow to do it. There's not much change in production from day to day. The Purchasing and Distribution departments have procedures to follow to accomplish any plan's objective. The assembly line, with automated equipment, is routine. Employees follow rules and procedures as well as fill out forms to communicate departmental needs.

Organizing Under Changing Conditions

To Roberta, a manager in a computer software company, organizing means a pragmatic approach to the rapid growth her company is experiencing. Who will be responsible for doing the record-keeping? Who will interface with the public? Who will get the product to the consumer and who will produce the product? Roberta intuitively understands the constant change going on in high growth situations. She can't expect a set procedure but she can implement a general network of employees who interact to accomplish the work goals. She knows she must delegate similar job responsibilities to employees. She knows that the employees' jobs have to be coordinated and she gives them the responsibility and authority to coordinate who needs to talk to whom, etc. The employees make many decisions to assure that the work flow continues. They can't rely on rules and procedures because every situation is different. Roberta's job is part doing and part supervising—making sure the flow of work and decisions accomplish the goals and objectives desired. To Roberta, organizing is how you coordinate the work that has been assigned to various employees.

Organizing: Is There One Best Way?

Tom and Roberta manage under different conditions: Tom has routine, stable, unchanging conditions; Roberta has changing, unstable, non-routine conditions. There is not one best way to organize, but there is one factor that can guide you in deciding how jobs will be coordinated. *Predictability* of the work means how much of the job is routine. If it's relatively stable and unchanging then procedures, policies and plans can be written down in manuals for employees to follow. Much of the decision-making is removed from the hands of employees and procedures guide the flow of work. If the work to be done is unpredictable with a lot of changes from day to day, then employees must make a lot of decisions to keep the flow of work going.

Under what conditions are you managing? How many of the jobs under your supervision are routine? How many jobs require coordination with other jobs? Does your department or work group coordinate with other work groups? Can you write a procedure to guide this communication? Can you rely on the abilities and decision-making of your subordinates? Can you devise a standard operating procedure (SOP)? If yes, do it. If no, train employees to communicate and coordinate.

Seven Advantages to Organizing

Poor organizing means poor management. Good organizing is the cornerstone to effective management.

1. ***Encourages a closer look at planning.*** We all have trouble stopping our frantic "doing" in order to plan. If you plan, you'll be doing little or no frantic "doing." Setting goals and formulating an action plan to accomplish those goals results in better organizing. Planning and organizing results in successful work groups.

2. ***Encourages a more efficient work group.*** You're not "putting out fires" any longer. Your work group runs smoothly. You and your subordinates don't have to "reinvent the wheel" every time a problem comes up. And, you're not losing time—lost time is lost money.

3. ***Assists in human resource planning.*** If you've organized according to the conditions within your work group, you know what kind of employees you need to hire and how to train the ones you have. If you have routine jobs with routine coordination needs, unskilled employees with average abilities can be hired. If you have non-routine jobs with non-routine coordination needs that require more decision-making by employees, then you should hire skilled, experienced, higher-ability employees.

4. ***Assists you in deciding how to lead.*** Leadership requires some flexibility on your part. Every employee needs a slightly different supervision style. Employees in routine jobs might only need encouragement and some monitoring from you. Employees in non-routine jobs might need more task direction as well as more encouragement from you.

5. ***Provides direction and guidance to employees.*** This is a benefit to any well-run work group. You have built into the work a degree of direction and feedback; therefore, you don't need to supervise or monitor as much as you would if you weren't organized.

6. ***Encourages you to delegate.*** Once you've set goals, devised an action plan, organized jobs and decided how they coordinate, you know the requirements of each job and you can delegate these jobs to subordinates with the abilities to successfully complete them. Managers are sometimes reluctant to delegate because they haven't done this organizing "homework." Delegation comes naturally once you've devised an action plan and made the organizing decisions.

7. ***Improves work group morale.*** You and your subordinates will experience a sense of satisfaction as members of a well-run work group. Frustration is seldom a problem.

Barriers to Organizing

Watch out for these tendencies to avoid organizing:

1. *It requires time and pre-planning.* Some managers don't like to plan because they don't see the inherent advantages of guidance, action plans and goal accomplishments.
2. *Chaos or "putting out fires" is mistaken for good management.* Some managers think it makes them look effective and competent when they ride up on the white horse and solve the problem. The opposite is true. The more smoothly your work group functions, the better you're managing. "Rescues" are kept to a minimum!
3. *Some situations or conditions don't appear to have the capacity for organizing.* Even non-predictability and constant change can be improved with some general organizing. Every situation has some degree of stable procedures. Hiring and training competent employees and giving them authority to make coordination decisions is an example of organizing.

A key relationship to remember is the connection between planning and organizing. Organizing has a plan as its reference point. The goals of the plan indicate what organizing must occur.

Eight Steps to Effective Organizing

1. Decide what jobs are needed to accomplish the objectives of the plan.
2. Decide how the jobs will be grouped into work units.
3. Decide how the jobs and/or work units must be coordinated within your department and between other departments.
4. Decide on formal relationships. Who reports to whom?
5. Decide how much authority must go with a job or work unit.
6. Decide who will make decisions and which decisions.
7. Delegate jobs or tasks to appropriately-selected employees.
8. Monitor results to accomplish the goals and objectives.

5

LEADING

What Is "Leading"?

Leadership is perhaps the most important managerial function you'll learn because it is through people that goals and objectives are accomplished. The way you manage or lead your employees determines the degree of success your unit, division and total organization will have.

Leadership is knowing your subordinates and what motivates them. It's knowing the motivating characteristics of jobs, tasks and projects. It's knowing the group dynamics of your work unit. It's the ability to teach, train, motivate, resolve conflicts, build an effective team and keep performance high.

What Does a Leader Do?

A leader is someone who plans, organizes, controls, communicates, delegates, coaches and accepts the responsibility for reaching the organization's goals. A leader has the authority and responsibility to accomplish the goals of her unit and is held accountable for the results. A leader is a manager.

What is Your Style?

There is not one best way to lead. You must determine how you want to deal with people. If it's effective, then it's your style.

Ann, a director in a government agency, spends much of her time setting the stage for her "leading." She meticulously plans what needs to be done. Her plans interconnect—her daily plans fit into her weekly plans which fit into her monthly plans. The long-range plans and their objectives were given to her by her boss. She breaks this annual plan down into small increments with the milestone marker approach. What needs to be done by March, by June, by September and by year-end? Then she knows what has to be done monthly to reach the annual objectives. After this action plan is set, she knows *what* to organize, *who* to organize and *how* to organize. Since the plans have a built-in control, she doesn't worry too much because she knows what and how to measure. For example, each employee has been assigned a set of tasks or a job. She's met with each subordinate and together they set mutually agreed-upon objectives. She'll informally chat with them and see how they're dong throughout the week or month. If they need help or assistance, she's available. She has an "open door" policy with them; they can pop in and touch base anytime. It's not a formal, "make an appointment" approach. She trained and developed her employees so they are more than able to accomplish their jobs. She is wise, she *delegated*. To her, delegation means that her employees do their jobs and problem-solve. They know they cannot dump the problem on her. She'll *help*, but they *do*! Ann is obviously a planner, allowing her to spend time walking around and being available for informal chats. She likes this interaction with her subordinates. They like her and respect her management ability. She knows every subordinate's family, career goals and little quirks.

What kind of a leader is Ann? She is both a task and social leader. She uses both leadership methods effectively. They work for her and fit her personality.

Greg, a product manager, does his planning much like Ann. Effective managers have to do this basic function. He has developed employees and delegated. Greg does this so he's free to spend more time planning long-range projects. Greg has a formal approach with subordinates. They make appointments if they need to see him. He doesn't feel comfortable spending informal time with his subordinates. Generally, Greg is the designer of the organization and he sets it in motion. His job is to deal with task or performance issues. He's solely a task-oriented leader. He's effective and it fits his personality.

Susie, a supervisor of a typing pool, doesn't plan much. She assumes her subordinates know what to do. Because she also does much of the typing, she mostly sees herself as a worker/supervisor. She likes the people she works with. Much time is spent socializing informally. She runs a "country club" group. She's a social-oriented leader. Unfortunately, this is not an effective style. The flow of work gets bottlenecked. The departments never get their typing back on a timely basis and it isn't accurate. Susie illustrates this ineffective leadership style. You can't be a social-oriented leader without also being a task-oriented leader.

Which style are you? Are you effective?

Nine Reasons for Employees' Poor Performance

1. The wrong job is given to the wrong employee—s/he isn't trained for it.
2. The wrong job is given to the wrong employee—s/he needs more challenge and you gave them a routine job which doesn't motivate them.
3. Subordinates need more training.
4. Subordinates are not involved in setting their own objectives and goals. You didn't communicate expectations.
5. Subordinates are not rewarded when they perform well; therefore, why should they excel?
6. Subordinates are not given support and guidance.
7. You're under-supervising.
8. You're over-supervising.
9. The goals and/or objectives are too high or too low.

Three Reasons the Department's Performance is Low

1. The nine employee-related reasons listed above.
2. You haven't *planned, organized, controlled* or *led*.
3. Poor goal-setting.

People Techniques to Improve Performance

1. **Reinforce** high performance as soon as you can. A praising remark, recognition and mentioning it in front of others are examples.
2. **Design jobs** so they have motivating characteristics. Giving authority and autonomy is one way. Delegating is another.
3. Be sure you have some **balance** or **effort** toward recognizing subordinates as people with needs that can be satisfied with proper job match or social interaction.
4. **Be fair** with employees. Respect their dignity.

6

CONFLICT WITHIN SELF: JOB vs. CAREER

Choosing a career is a key decision you must make. If you avoid a conscious choice, you can experience a conflict within yourself. Unresolved conflict is stressful, hinders your effectiveness and can make you appear uncommitted, indecisive and in need of direction. By not choosing a career you can get locked out of advancement. What is the difference between a job and a career?

Career Orientation Is...

Career orientation is a long-term commitment to yourself. It's a desire to map out a path that guides you today, next month, in five years and in 10 years. It's an attitude you acquire that helps you focus on learning skills, acquiring conceptual processes and broadening your aspirations for the accomplishment of the career goals you've set. It's the attitude that your current job is only a stepping stone to your next job. In short, it's the conscious choice to advance through the ranks of management by acquiring skills, attitudes and behaviors that will be recognized and rewarded by promotion.

Job Orientation Is...

Job orientation is, by its nature, a short-term and somewhat narrow focus on technical skills, task completion and job performance. It's an "8 to 5" commitment for five days a week. Its further focus is on the specialist and detail aspects of the job. If you do not make a conscious choice between a *career* and a *job*, the default result may be to stay locked in at your current level.

Six Factors That Hinder Career Choice

1. *Locked into satisfying others and neglecting yourself.* Not knowing your needs, wants, life and professional goals. Time constraints and family demands can distract you. "Old tapes" can keep you from giving yourself permission to satisfy yourself.
2. *Lack of career role models in your organization.* Women in responsible positions can inspire and guide your efforts, help you see your options.
3. *Short-term thinking.* For example, current financial requirements may hinder you from looking beyond today, this week or next year.
4. *Misunderstanding.* A job is not a career.
5. *Uncertainty of the future in your private life.* Where will you be next year?
6. *Security-focused.* It's risky to choose because then you must commit. Fear of the unknown. A career might be too challenging, too demanding. You may have to change. Fear of failure. Fear of role shifting.

Six Advantages of the Career Choice

1. *Career orientation means promotions.*
2. *Career orientation is goal-directed.* You leave confusion and conflict behind you. You devise an action plan that guides you. You're free from "drifting" and indecision.
3. *More satisfaction and fulfillment from working.* You're not locked into the potential boredom of a dead-end job. Opportunities for growth are on the horizon.
4. *Broadens your contacts.* You interact with interesting people. You might access circles to which you aspire, whether social or intellectual.
5. *You gain independence, autonomy and responsibility.*
6. *You gain financial rewards.*

7

BEING LIKED vs.
BEING EFFECTIVE

Everyone wants to be liked. Being liked is great for the ego—it can help you establish a strong referent power base. However, many women managers tend to be totally unaware that their *main* motive is to be liked. They can slowly erode their credibility when subordinates pick up on this. And they do! If you show any reluctance to confront poor performance, to delegate a messy task or to show your authority, you'll become ineffective. Don't trade being respected for being liked. You don't need to trade off! You *can* be both and you *must* be respected above all else. You may need to confront a subordinate and, in the short run, they will possibly be angry. But, in the long run, they'll get over the anger and become productive. And...they'll respect you due to the confrontation.

8

YOU CAN'T IGNORE THE POLITICAL SYSTEM

The political aspects of organizations are inherently tied to the informal organization, your personal power and influence, and the "Old Boy" network. A manager must be skilled at influencing, compromising and collaborating in order to achieve personal, departmental and organizational goals. You'll need to learn how to develop the network of mutual obligations with others. You may need to build coalitions to gain support for decisions or activities you're engaged in. You need to develop your personal power of influence to be effective personally and professionally. Getting in the "Old Boy" network helps you and your department become effective and productive.

A real dilemma for many women is that building power, political connections, informal networks and coalitions is not a familiar activity. Many women lack experience. Also, many women have an attitude dilemma. Power and politics may be perceived as a negative process. You'll need to discard that belief if you're going to be effective. Perhaps learning about the positive aspects of the organization and your department's goal achievements will assist you in changing this attitude dilemma.

Building networks of mutual obligations with others is the name of the game. If you don't plan, you can't win. Winning means you, your work group and other people in other work groups are more efficient, effective and productive. In short, the organization wins when goals get accomplished with less effort. If your department is effective, you win and advance.

Use the Informal Organization

Management is not an individual sport—managing is the process of utilizing people from the informal and formal organization to accomplish goals. It's a team attitude—you need others for not only goal accomplishment but for support, guidance, direction and advancement. You'll need to tap into the political informal networking system and learn appropriate behaviors if you want to be effective for your organization and advancement.

What Is the Informal Organization?

The informal organization is that network of people that you won't find on the organizational chart—but it's where the real action is. Joe may be the official supervisor and have the supervisory position, but Karen, a worker in Joe's department, has the real power to get things done. You don't neglect Joe, but it's Karen you go to. Why? There are many sources of power in organizations and positional power is only one. Karen may have an expert, information, referent, reward power or influence base. For example, Karen may possess information you need to accomplish your group's objective. If you and Karen are part of an informal network of mutual obligation, then she'll be a great asset in your department. If not, then information may be withheld or mysteriously slow in coming. It's a fact of organizational life that things get done through the informal system. Reciprocal obligations help you immeasurably.

Six Advantages of Informal Networking

1. It helps you and your group accomplish your work unit's goals.
2. It makes the necessary coordination between work units easier.
3. It provides a set of people who support, guide and direct you.
4. It fosters improvement in your interpersonal skills.
5. It improves your promotability when you're viewed by others as savvy to organizational life.
6. It broadens your perspective so you see the big picture, and consequently improves your management skills.

How can you learn to use the informal organization and establish a reciprocal network system for you and your department?

Six Steps to Establish Informal Networks

1. *Move around the organization.* Looking for groups that can provide your department with needed resources (information, services, personnel, etc.)
2. *Become acquainted with people in these groups.*
3. *Never let a chance go by.* Always indicate your appreciation of something a group did for you.
4. *Be attentive and do a favor.* They will reciprocate.
5. *Conduct yourself in a friendly, professional and confident manner.* Be sincere in your reciprocal actions.
6. *Broaden out and start looking for other signals.* Look for indications of informal leadership or power. After awhile you'll not only tune in and figure out who you need to know to accomplish your group's objectives, but also who you need to know to gain personal power and advancement. The effective manager utilizes the informal network...and it's *okay*. It's of mutual benefit and no one gets hurt. This networking process also helps you avoid the "detail mentality" of your job. Again, you're perceived as a "big picture" person with initiative and organizational savvy. And you are, indeed, doing your job better and more efficiently.

How to Acquire More Personal Power

Power *is not* negative. Some people tend to say they are opposed to power, but perhaps that's because they don't know how to formally get it. It's a simple idea: Power is interpersonal influence. To get it, you find what it is that you have others might want. Women have always had much informal power but little formal power. Give yourself permission to be direct and acquire personal influence in both the formal and informal sense. Personal influence and power are necessary skills to acquire. According to French and Raven (1959), there are six bases of social power.

Six Sources of Personal Influence and Power

1. *Legitimate Power* is based on the authority of the position one holds. Example: You have influence because you have the job.
2. *Reward Power* is the ability to compensate and give rewards for completed tasks or favors. Examples of rewards are money, public praise, promotion, acceptance and attention.
3. *Coercive Power* is the ability to punish. It's based on fear and the perception that subordinates will be punished if they don't conform. Withholding valued resources or emotional support from others are examples. Another example: You are the data processing

expert and others do things for you and your department because you may not give them valued reports on time.

4. **Referent Power** is based on the attractiveness and appeal of individuals that causes them to be liked personally. Referent power is effective for women in non-traditional occupations because it has not been sex-role stereotyped as either a masculine or feminine power base. Women with referent power are respected for their competence and personal characteristics regardless of their formal authority. Example: Others respond to your requests because they like you.

5. **Expert Power** is the influence given to a manager who has superior knowledge, ability or skill. This base can be derived from special training, experience, holding of information, exceptional skill or just overall competence. Example: You influence others because they need your expertise.

6. **Information Power** is the influence people have when they hold information that others need and want. Example: The secretary who can get you in to see the boss by keeping you informed about his schedule will have power and influence over you.

Managers need additional authority and power to be effective and advance. Personal influence is, in many ways, more important than formal authority. Women should recognize the value of power. It must be accompanied with competence or it is but a short-lived phenomenon.

Use your power productively and effectively. You should work toward a balance between the use of the extreme, coercive, ''throwing your weight around'' power and the referent base of ''being liked.''

Getting Into the "Old Boy" Network

Some women complain about how this network is blocked to them. They never seem to be invited to the formal or informal social functions. Breaking into the areas of influence traditionally dominated by men is possible, but difficult. In some companies, getting accepted by the influential managers is open and based on merit. Like any social grouping, you must have a utility or exchange value in order to be included. In other companies merit, competence, exchange value and being male are the criteria. Many women have reported that it isn't necessarily the physical exclusion from the interaction with the network that hinders their advancement, but the lack of information they receive. The network has what they need—such as who's doing what, what plans are in the making, who's about to get fired, who offended whom, who did a great job, what the key decision-makers are considering and personal details such as the boss's spouse was just promoted, had a baby, won an award, etc. *Information is influence* and getting it is what matters.

Eight Ways to be Included in the "Old Boy" Network

1. Demonstrate self-confidence and initiative.
2. Acquire the behaviors and traits of successful managers (i.e. savvy of the informal organization, knowing the Big Picture, being a direct communicator, flexibility, problem-solving, being a team member, knowing politics, having a high profile, etc.).
3. Know your organization from top to bottom (how it works, how things get done, how it's organized, strategic plans, etc.).
4. Personally know as many of the "movers and shakers" as you can.
5. Establish mutliple reciprocal networks with others (it's effective for you and your department, and some of these relationships may be with individuals who get promoted to the top).
6. Get psychological support from informal women's groups (inside and outside).
7. Get involved in activities that gain their attention (high visibility projects, task forces, etc.).
8. Become indispensable to their success on key projects (i.e. you're the best planner or organizer and they need you; you have a friend from an earlier network that's been promoted to the president's staff, you add an extra element to the project—in addition to competence—that they value such as a good sense of humor, good people skills to keep everyone motivated, etc.).

Entering can come via a male or female network partner. Entry can come through any of the power or personal influence bases. Such bases are: 1) they like and admire you and your people skills 2) they perceive you as someone who can cause trouble so they co-opt you 3) you have the ability to reward them—such as disseminating information, resources, budget allocation, extra personnel, etc. 4) you're an expert in an area which needs assistance 5) you occupy a key management position.

You must be persistent, subtly demonstrating competence, effectiveness, productivity and the ability to advance. The network members must see you as a competent "mover and shaker" with potential to contribute to the group.

Examples of Getting Into a Network

Judith is an upper-level manager in a large insurance company. She's competent, effective and a high achiever. She's an example of a manager who's acquired most of the skills of managing. Judith has found the style of management that fits her personality. She doesn't think of herself as a *woman* manager, but solely as *a* manager. She got in an "Old Boy" group early and has been promoted upward with many of them. How? She likes and enjoys the same type of informal, outside-of-work activities the men do. She goes to football games, plays golf, swims, works out at the gym and goes to lunch with her colleagues. She's fun to be around. She's in on what's going on, and she and her department get things done more easily because of this.

Karen is a top manager in a telecommunications firm. She's competent, productive and also effective. Judith and Karen are on even ground regarding their managerial behaviors. Karen has a reserved personality and her management style fits her personality. Karen doesn't enjoy the same things the men do outside of work. She's more comfortable keeping work separate from her social life. She's in an "Old Boy" network and is advancing along with them. How? They need the resources that she controls; she assigns personnel to their projects. She always assigns the top performers, not the average performers, to their projects. In exchange, she is kept informed of what's going on and other valued information that she needs to plan more effectively. Their jobs and her job are made easier by this reciprocal behavior.

9

BEING DISCOUNTED
IN GROUPS

When a woman is in a group of men, she is likely to be isolated. This phenomenon is not necessarily a function of the individuals involved but a function of the group dynamics. Consequently, women must be aware of the ramifications of sex differences in groups.

**Four Strategies to Increase Your Group Credibility
and Performance**

1. Seek out role models in powerful positions in your own organization or in other organizations. These role models can provide you with specific advice. Also, you can refer to them in your all-male group and *by association* you may be able to change any negative stereotyping of you.
2. Another strategy involves acquiring a knowledge of strong communication speech and body language patterns. Your credibility can be enhanced by eliminating certain speech patterns such as the habit of swinging your voice tone upward at the end of a spoken statement. Doing this transforms it into a question. This speech habit creates the impression that you're uncertain and you risk losing credibility.
3. Do your homework. Be prepared to discuss the agenda items with confidence and self-assuredness. If you can go beyond what the

others may know, you can establish credibility early. Once established, it's much easier to maintain.

4. The above strategy involves using the expert base of personal power and influence. Another strategy to increase your effectiveness in groups is to use another of the typical bases of power. You can easily use referent power if they like and enjoy your personality. The expert power base is effective when you have depth and breadth of knowledge or skill in an area that the group needs expertise. Reward power is effective if the members of the group see you as having the ability to give a compliment, raise, information, support or other valued response.

10

PROFESSIONAL IMAGE: VOICE AND BODY COMMUNICATIONS

Voice Credibility

Women do have some unique, characteristic speech patterns that sometimes distract from their credibility. A few are covered to illustrate. Women tend to use *adjectives* which add little meaning (such as "incredible," "great," "wonderful," "divine") but cost a lot in terms of credibility. Women also connect *little questions* on the end of declarative sentences that can be interpreted as uncertainty. This habit also discounts comments—"It's time to get down to work, don't you think?" Some women have a habit of swinging the *tone upward* at the end of spoken statements, making them questions. Some use a lot of *modifying* phrases such as "maybe," "sort of," "it could be." There is also a tendency to use *disclaimers* preceding opinions such as, "I may be wrong, but I believe we've spent enough time discussing that issue." These disclaimers invite a challenge. Some women are artists at removing their own authority by using *apologies* such as, "I'm really incredibly sorry bothering you because you're probably overloaded, but I'd sort of like to ask, could you check your report for errors?" Would it not have been more direct and effective to say, "Check this report for errors"?

Body Language Credibility

Women tend to use body language that unbeknownst to them, communicates a second-class status or less power. A tendency to hold the head slightly downward to avoid a direct stare, avoiding direct eye contact, rounding shoulders and more-than-necessary smiles and nods are but a few patterns to avoid. Men and women read these body signals subconsciously which leads to discounting of even the most persuasive, credible verbal comments. Enroll in a course at a college or university, go to a seminar or read books about nonverbal communication. You can increase your power tenfold by modifying a few body language patterns.

Professional Image—Clothing

We are judged by many factors—one of them is how we dress. We need to make credible first impressions. We need to look self-assured and assertive. Avoid the too cute or too pretty look. You need to look like a manager and clothing is one cue that others respond to.

How can you project an image that is professional? There is no absolute standard. You must rely on your assessment of what is appropriate in your company and industry. Select a person who is generally admired and respected, and follow his or her lead.

In many organizations, you need to look like a manager. This may be a frivolous but necessary part of the job. When others observe you, they're making many conclusions about you such as your economic level, educational level, social position, sophistication level, credibility, management potential and others. Again, the corporate dress must be determined by your assessment. Generally, it will be a conservative look—avoid faddish clothing. A conservative wardrobe can be expensive; however, it's money well spent. Also, conservative items can weather the fashion shifts and be worn several years. You don't need a lot of clothing if you're creative. A couple of navy and neutral colored suits can be modified dramatically with the addition of different blouses and scarves.

For additional assistance, many department stores have personal shopping service personnel who are trained in image dressing. It's a free service and once you find a personal shopper that you like, she can become your personal consultant on image dressing. Don't be intimidated by approaching a personal shopper; but do make an appointment, if possible, so that she can spend quality time with you. Every year I organize a workshop for my executive M.B.A. students and I've never been disappointed by the eagerness of the personal shoppers I've contacted. These people are thrilled to have a woman walk in who needs their help. They also can help accessorize your current wardrobe, coordinating your current items with new ones.

11

BEING PASSED OVER AT PROMOTION TIME

This is always a disappointment, but you can turn it into an opportunity! Why did it happen? The answer may provide you with new goals and direction. Let's look at some possible reasons.

Prime Source: Your Boss

Ask your boss why you didn't get the job. Many bosses say, "No one had any idea that you wanted to be considered for the promotion." If this is the case, you may have failed in communicating your desire to people who may someday be in a position to help you, including your boss.

If you're fortunate, your boss will be honest. If you have any deficiencies, you'll be told. Remember...feedback is critical for your development. It might feel like criticism but it's good information to seek and use. A lot of the time you won't get honest feedback, but vague comments such as, "The other candidates were better suited for the job." Probe, be firm and ask for specifics on what you can do to improve your chances. Whatever information you get, evaluate it to see if you can increase your promotability.

Prime Source: Yourself

Ask yourself these questions:

1. Do I possess the key traits of successful people such as initiative, flexibility, self-direction, confidence, team spirit, interpersonal influence and system knowledge?
2. Do I demonstrate the skills of good management? Can I plan, control, organize and lead?
3. Do I sell myself? Do others see me as credible, competent and effective? Have I gained visibility with those who make decisions?
4. Do I fit into the norms of the company? Am I dressing appropriately? Am I cooperative or competitive—whichever fits my company's culture?
5. Have I thrown away the barriers of the "old tapes"? Can I be flexible? Do I delegate and trust others to do a good job? Am I trading being liked for effectiveness? Am I too detailed, and technical? Do I lack the broad view?
6. Have I communicated to others that I want a career path in this company?
7. Do I lack credentials? Do I have the education necessary for the next position?
8. Have I offended someone? Did I make a mistake somewhere?

If the answers suggest that you need to add some self-improvement to your plan, remedy the problem area.

Prime Source: Others

Ask peers and those you trust for feedback and suggestions. It is helpful to get another perspective.

The Big Reason

Sometimes companies don't promote women. Such organizations have a pattern that you can observe. Are there women in the management ranks? Are they all on the entry or first level? A quick review of where the women are tells you what your chances for advancement are. Your company can't say you were passed over because you're female—that's illegal. However, they can say you lack the proper skills when, in fact, you may not. Also, observe how males treat women or talk about them. This may indicate to you that you must face a decision. Do you stay in the dead-end position or map out tactics to get another job? If you move to another company, check it out by informally asking whether women are represented on the various levels of management so you don't repeat the same dead-end scenario.

12

SUPERVISING MEN

Supervising men can be difficult for the woman manager. Some men will have many misgivings about working for a woman. Here are some examples:

Five Typical Scenarios and How to Deal with Them

1. *Men may not know how to treat you.* Consequently, you'll need to take the initiative. In short, you need to establish your credibility. If the situation is particularly awkward, set up a meeting and explain what your objectives for the work unit are, how they fit in and how you want to be treated. A good method is to use the standby, "Treat me like you would any male supervisor." Another good one is, "Treat me like a human supervisor." Basic things may need to be covered such as "When I'm at the door first, I'll open it and if you're there first you open it," or "If I can't lift a box, I'll appreciate your help."
2. *Male subordinates may be concerned whether you can play the political game or use the informal system.* This is because they don't know if you have the power to help them if they need it. If you've done your homework it shouldn't be difficult to demonstrate that you know the people who have power and influence in the organization and how to access it. No one said that you can't drop names, either. References to a meeting with Mr. Top Boss or a conversation with Ms. Division Head or lunch with Mr. Department Chief calms this fear.

3. **Men may treat you like a mother figure.** I wouldn't get into this role because you never know what they expect from their mother. Also, it can lead to being taken advantage of. For example, "Could you finish this for me?" or "I might be late," or "I really don't want to do that job." However, if you feel comfortable nurturing *all* your subordinates and that's your basic leadership style, it may work for you.

4. **Men may treat you with disrespect or a condescending attitude.** Confront this behavior immediately—the longer you let it go, the worse it becomes, the harder it is to talk to them and other subordinates begin to lose respect for you. One method I've used is assertive in the sense that you're respecting yourself *and* them...say, "You may not be aware of it, Joe, but you're behaving as if you don't like and respect me. You don't have to like me, but I expect all my subordinates to show respect for me and my position. Organizations can't function if respect for authority is missing. If you don't know what behavior I'm referring to, we can discuss it on Friday." Usually this works, however, there are times when they really don't know that they're being disrespectful. If this is the case, point out each instance as it occurs and do it privately. Reprimanding in public can backfire on you.

5. **In this situation some men are just a lost cause.** If you're too professional, they'll complain. If you're too warm, they'll complain. Your job is to find a good balance and stick to it. Be competent, direct, goal-oriented and hope for the best. You can't overcome every man's hang-up. That's his job!

13

SEXUAL HARRASSMENT AND SEXISM

Sexual Harassment

Sexual harassment is any unwanted behavior that interferes with the ability to work in an atmosphere free of intimidation. In its more severe form it creates an implicit or explicit condition for employment and promotion. It's an ugly game some men with more power than you will play. It can be subtle or coercive pressure for sexual activity. It's demeaning and frightening to the woman involved.

A Seven-Step Strategy for Dealing With Harassment

1. Talk privately to him and tell him you're not interested and to stop; confront *early*.
2. Tell others, especially a trusted senior man, what is happening and elicit their support.
3. Keep a detailed log of what is said, when, where, under what circumstances.
4. Write a letter to be placed in your personnel file.
5. Contact your supervisor or, if the person harassing you is your supervisor, go one level up and explain what is going on. Indicate you've documented it and have witnesses. (Imply you may have to go to the Equal Employment Opportunity Commission if it's not stopped.)

6. As a final step you may find it necessary to sue and you're well within your rights to do so.
7. Above all, don't feel afraid or helpless. Most companies are run by decent people who will not tolerate such behavior.

To help avoid such encounters, maintain professional, job-related behaviors. There are a few power abusers out there, but don't let them spoil your excitement and involvement in work!

Sexism Is Still Alive

There are indeed overtly biased men and women in the workplace. Unless they have extreme power to make or break your career, ignore them because they are going to dig their own graves. It's no longer socially acceptable to be outwardly and verbally biased. It's the covert bias that causes you the most trouble. Generally, most biased comments, behaviors and attitudes are not known by the sender. In fact, when you confront them they're surprised that you are offended. My advice is to avoid direct confrontation because they become defensive and project the situation onto your behavior. Then you get tagged as the "bad guy." Go into every situation as a person with dignity and self-worth. Acquire the attitude, personal characteristics and behaviors of an effective manager/person. Learn the functions of management. You are a professional—behave like one. Develop a knowledge of your total organization, its functional areas, products or services, competitive situation, people to know and personal base of influence. There is only one way to combat bias— prove that it's not accurate by your personal actions, attitudes and effectiveness.

14

REACTOR TO PLANNER

Disadvantages of Not Planning

You can put out fires and wait for the next crisis if you want. You can waste time when you and your subordinates don't quite know what the goals are, what the performance criteria is or what the plan is. You can make excuses to your boss why the project is late, why the costs are high and why it isn't accurate. Or, you can choose to stop *reacting* to your work and start *planning* for the future...of today, tomorrow, next week and even next month.

From Reactor to Planner. You can wait and react to what circumstances present themselves or you can discipline yourself and manage your environment by planning. New supervisors are not aware of the multitude of tasks, projects, opportunities, problems and crises that can present themselves. Mostly, they're not aware that planning is the key function of management. Plans set goals and objectives. Plans give guidance not only for *where* we're going but for *how* we're going to get there. Planning is the framework of management. Planning precedes organizing, controlling and leading. It begins at the top levels of organizations and ends with the individual work unit. Obviously, the new supervisor must be aware of the segmented nature of her planning and how it fits into the objectives of the organization.

Let's review the planning basics for the supervisory level. The new supervisor must face the reality of doing something she has little experience in, must overcome the specialist orientation of previous jobs and learn the basics of planning. Fortunately, planning on the supervisory level is not broad; it is specific enough to allow a new supervisor to rely on already-acquired skills.

Supervisors must plan before all other functions can occur. You must develop a course of action (based on data, future expectations, changes, etc.) before all else. For example, how can you organize your work unit without a plan? How can you staff and schedule your subordinates without a plan? How can you lead without knowing the path? Finally, how can you control the results without a plan to implement and measure them?

Planning for the supervisor is short-range. A supervisor will plan for only six months, one month, one week or even just one day. The scheduling of a unit's production line employees is short-range planning. Also, the scheduling of preventive maintenance on equipment may be several months in advance but still within the short-range time period.

Five Steps to a Planner

Your job requires the ability to plan for the future (one day to six months or more). Planning is required in many areas—the following are only some examples: quality of output, quantity of output, cost control, use of human resources, use of equipment resources, attendance, customer satisfaction, and employee training and development. The planning process involves five steps.

1. Establish objectives for each area of responsibility. For example, three new accountants must be hired.
2. Develop a scenario of possible future events that might influence the attainment of objectives. For example, the labor pool may be limited, you cannot find qualified accountants or your pay scale may be low.
3. Decision-making
   a. What are the possible alternate courses of action?
      - Advertise in an accountants' periodical.
      - Ask personal friends to recruit for you.
      - Interview on college campuses.
      - Ask for a salary adjustment for the position.
   b. Evaluate each course of action. Which would accomplish more?
   c. Select the best Action Plan. Advertising may help as well as campus recruiting. Also, salary adjustment assists accomplishment of the objective.
4. Implement the Action Plan.

5. Evaluate the results to determine if your goal has been accomplished. If so, it's the end of this plan. If not, you'll need to go over your ideas again. The key question? Can you become a planner instead of a reactor?

15

SEE THE BIG PICTURE: A SPECIALIST TO A GENERALIST

A common problem we face is the transition from the specialist with a "technical" job to a generalist with a broad-view management job. Before entering management you typically have a technical, specialized, narrowly-focused job which demands a specialist orientation. As you enter management you must broaden your perspective to a generalist orientation. You must leave the detail orientation and see the "big picture."

Not Letting Go of the Technical Job

Karen was the best accountant that the department ever had. She was a hard worker and knew the department better than the other accountants. When a supervisory position opened up, Karen was promoted. She continued working hard and, as before, was somewhat of a perfectionist. Although her work group had an average performance record, she was still considered a capable supervisor. After some time, she began to lose personnel because they quit or transferred to other departments. Her subordinates complained that she felt she could do any job better than anyone; therefore, she never delegated the more challenging accounts—she kept doing them herself. When the company began to grow and she had to coordinate more with other functional areas, she didn't know what information they needed, when they needed it or how to coordinate. Karen was stuck in her technical, specialist mindset. Karen was also stuck in her current job. She continued to rely on her technical skills instead of broadening into the use of management skills. She continued her technical work when what she really needed was to learn to plan, organize, lead and coordinate. Karen did not develop the ability to see how each job fit into the larger pattern of the department or how her department fit into the larger organization. She didn't learn how each job contributes to the goal accomplishment of the department and how the department contributes to the goals of the total organization. She didn't acquire the broad, generalist orientation of management.

Karen needed to learn about the total organization and the "big picture." At the very least, she needed to develop short-term planning and implementation skills. Specialists have a difficult time becoming effective in supervisory positions; consequently, they don't climb the ladder as readily as generalists.

What are some key advantages to seeing the "big picture"?

Five Advantages of a Generalist Orientation

1. It encourages delegation.
2. It encourages planning.
3. It encourages organization.
4. It encourages learning and acquisition of effective management skills.
5. It encourages you to develop and train yourself and your subordinates for advancement and efficiency.

Some key barriers holding you back from seeing the "big picture."

Barriers

1. Self-absorption in technical skills.
2. Reluctance to try new behaviors or risk making mistakes.
3. The "I can do it better" fallacy. (This barrier comes from the perfectionism we must overcome to leave the "doer" role behind.)
4. Lack of knowledge about how to acquire a generalist orientation.

16

FOLLOWER TO LEADER

The tendency to follow is something the new supervisor must always be aware of. Why is this? Leading requires many skills that may need to be learned by a newly-appointed supervisor. Planning, organizing and staffing are prerequisites of effective leadership—they are interrelated. In planning you need to know your subordinates' needs, expectations, qualifications, limits and personal objectives. Should they be involved in setting objectives? What jobs can you delegate to them? Are you a participative leader or a more autocratic, controlling leader? Should you modify your style to fit the employee? It is easy to fall into the trap of asking your boss for direction. This follower orientation does not endear you to your boss. You must take the initiative to act. You must not be a follower, but a leader. To do so requires acquisition of the conceptual, human relations, administrative and technical skills of management. You probably already have the technical skills if you were promoted from within the unit. The administrative skills of planning, organizing and controlling are acquired by studying the basics and practicing. The human relations skills of leadership are also acquired skills. The conceptual skills involve the ability to acquire, analyze and interpret information. These skills involve being able to understand the conditions of your unit, department and total organization. I encourage you to think broadly and expand your skills...take the initiative and lead!

You can't wait for direction from your boss. Your department's success depends on your confidence and ability to leave the follower behind. Seizing the leader role may hinge on some internal barriers as well as situational barriers.

Five Steps to Leadership

1. Give yourself permission to lead.
2. Discard "old tapes" that interfere. For example, if you tend to avoid offering new suggestions, reprogram yourself to accept risk as part of managing.
3. Arm yourself with the skills of planning, organizing and controlling.
4. Acquire traits of successful people. Which do you already have? Capitalize on them.
5. Make it easier on yourself—pick someone who's an effective leader and emulate her behavior. Ask her advice when needed.

17

DELEGATION

Delegating is perhaps the most difficult task for the supervisor. You must learn that you're no longer a "doer," but a "delegator."

You can no longer utilize the "if I work harder" mentality. Your "doing" is not going to be effective. You need to work through the efforts of others to accomplish goals. You'll need to risk trusting your subordinates to achieve. Letting go and depending on others to do a job that you are accountable for is difficult. The success or failure of this process depends on the personality and style of leadership of the superior. Some bosses will delegate a task but give no authority to accomplish it. Some supervisors are particularly vulnerable to the "failing to delegate trap" because of their fear of risk, desire for perfection, "doer" orientation or other limiters. Also, attitudes formed about supervisory behavior can constrain effective supervision such as "supervisors dump all the work on subordinates, therefore I won't do that," or "supervisors are lazy, I'll be a working supervisor." In addition, new supervisors may fear being disliked by subordinates.

It has been mentioned that you need to avoid the "detail" trap and develop a "big picture" mentality. Knowing your organization's goals and industry, networking and understanding political realities will assist you in your transition to supervisor. Knowing what delegation actually is, how to do it, the benefits and destructive aspects if you don't delegate will convince you that you can't ignore this necessity.

Seven Processes in Delegation

1. Delegation is the process of *assigning* certain tasks to each subordinate so that each has a specific job to perform. Routine tasks can be assigned to any employee. Some tasks, projects or functions can only be assigned to those subordinates who are qualified. Hence the necessity of knowing, developing and training your employees becomes evident.

2. Delgation is also *granting authority* to a subordinate to act and make decisions within prescribed limits. You must let your employees know how far their authority extends. For example, if you assign the task of ordering routine office supplies, the employee needs to know which suppliers they can order from, whether to get competitive bids, whether to order weekly or monthly and what suppliers are acceptable. If you don't tell them the limits, they'll be in a guessing mode that only creates problems for everyone.

3. Delegation is also creating a *sense of responsibility* in the employee to perform the task adequately. This process can be a motivating factor to the employee.

4. Delegation requires another new and unfamiliar task called *planning*. Once more, the supervisor must learn another skill. No one really likes planning until one has enjoyed its benefits or experienced the chaos of not planning. Planning requires thought about exactly what has to be done, how to divide it, how to assign it, who to delegate it to, how to explain it, how to establish standards of performance, how to direct it and how to control or measure the results. New supervisors can get trapped early by disorganization, overload of work, urgency and crises—usually because they didn't plan, organize, delegate or control. The early months of the new supervisor's tenure are stressful, but if you do your homework (literally) you can provide a smoother work flow.

5. In spite of these processes of delegation, *the accountability and responsibility is not delegated*; hence the supervisor's potential conflict can occur: "How can I risk the possibility of failure on their part when I'm the one who'll get blamed?" Some new supervisors must be particularly aware of their tendency to hold on to special assignments or projects because of the potential risk, the potential of failure or the potential that the employees won't do as good a job. If the "pleasing others" trap, the "trying harder" trap or the "being perfect" trap is operating, the possibility of becoming overextended, overwhelmed and overstressed is there. Also, a tendency to check and recheck all dele-

gated tasks can be destructive to your effectiveness, your department's effectiveness, and your subordinate's morale and motivation. One or two instances of compulsive "looking over your subordinate's shoulders" will send a message you might not want to send. They perceive (probably correctly) that you're compulsive, don't trust them, don't think they're competent and won't ever think anything they do is good enough. As a leader you want to avoid this! Don't over-supervise!

6. If you don't delegate anything but the routine things, you will become not only overwhelmed, but you'll also be failing in your function as a leader whose responsibility is to *develop and motivate your subordinates*. As a leader, you need to know your employees well enough to assess their capabilities for special tasks, and then *use* them!

7. *When should you do it yourself?* This is always a key question. Unfortunately, there is not an absolute answer. It depends so much on the nature of the actual work of the department. Many experts suggest that a line supervisor should not do the actual work of the unit or department more than 15-25 percent of the time. But, there are obvious times when a supervisor may do the actual work such as 1) trying out a new procedure or equipment 2) instructing or training subordinates 3) during temporary overload situations.

Seven Steps to Effective Delegation

1. Analyze the project that needs to be accomplished, set up standards for results and control.
2. Divide the project into significant units that can be delegated.
3. Know your subordinates, their qualifications, expertise, needs, etc.
4. Decide who will be assigned a unit.
5. Have a plan of action on how you will explain it to them.
6. Explain standards of expectation and limits of authority.
7. Have a plan of directing or coaching if they need it, but use it only when needed.

Five Advantages of Delegation

1. It provides a mechanism on which to build trust.
2. The department can get more done.
3. Your subordinates are developed, trained and challenged.
4. It is a vehicle to start building a team.

5. It allows you time to do and develop the real supervisory jobs of planning, building a team, scheduling, motivating, coaching, leading, training, controlling results and coordinating jobs, projects inside your department or between departments.

Delegation gives you time: 1) to develop the skills of managing 2) to gain the "big picture" 3) to be seen as an effective manager because you will be an effective manager. Remember, management is getting goals accomplished through others. It's their performance that you'll be evaluated on. Entry into supervision must be accomplished by this single concept. For the first time, it's not your doing that's being evaluated, but your ability to get subordinates to do.

18

DECISION-MAKING AND PROBLEM-SOLVING

Decision-making and problem-solving are key processes that require a supervisor's attention daily. They are learned skills that ask the supervisor to draw on her knowledge of her department's objectives as well as those of the organization. The two processes are obviously related; one requiring the other. The basic decision-making and problem-solving cycle is *recognition*, *solution*, *implementation* and *outcome evaluation*.

What Is a Problem?

A problem is the gap between what is at this moment and what is desired in the future. It's what is off-target or unwanted. Sharon, a production supervisor, recognized a problem when the 8 a.m. shift began and three workers were absent. The assembly line would be shut down if she didn't solve the problem quickly. What are her options? Call others in on overtime? Keep three over from the night shift? Set up for another product that requires less workers? What are the tradeoffs? The first two result in extra labor costs. The last one results in downtime to set up for the other product plus the downtime to set up for the first product again. And, downtime costs. Which product is needed for filling rush orders? Losing customers if rush orders aren't met also costs. Which option costs the most?

Which is priority? She had options. She needed to decide which was the best choice. Her decision was to keep three from the night shift and pay overtime. Implement the option? Notify three to stay. Outcome evaluation? Costs were minimized and workers needed the extra pay. This was a simple problem, but more complex ones can fool you. Indentifying the actual problem from the symptoms takes much analysis. A department's decrease in productivity, low morale, conflict between people and groups, an organization's loss of market share, falling stock prices and profit decrease are more complex. Identification of the cause of these problems can be difficult. Without knowing the cause, generating solutions is even more difficult.

Six Basic Steps to Problem-Solving

1. ***Problem identification.*** Write a few sentences describing the situation as you see it. Who, what, how and when? How are the people involved contributing to the problem?
2. ***Objectives.*** What would the problem look like if it were resolved? What is the desired result? What objectives do you want to accomplish? What would the behavior of people be if the situation is resolved?
3. ***Solutions.*** Generate a list of action plans that may resolve the problem and meet the objectives.
4. ***Decision.*** Analyze, evaluate and select the most feasible plan.
5. ***Implement.***
6. ***Evaluate.*** Did the action plan resolve the problem? If yes, continue. If no, repeat the steps.

Barriers to Decision-Making and Problem-Solving

1. Worrying about what others think.
2. Letting others decide.
3. Outcome is uncertain.
4. Fear of failure.
5. Thinking there's a perfect solution.
6. Too much perceived responsibility and accountability.
7. Wanting perfect information.
8. Thinking you can please everyone.
9. Thinking the problem will resolve itself.
10. Having too many other problems.
11. Not recognizing that a problem exists.

19

PROMOTION OVER PEERS AND ESTABLISHING CREDIBILITY

Getting promoted over your peers and then managing them can be a difficult situation. This is because they may resent being passed over or perhaps sense the loss of you as a friend. You need tact and a direct approach. Immediately, discuss with them what has happened. A direct approach is better than an indirect one or avoiding the situation altogether. If you wait, a problem can develop and then you have a mess to untangle. Tell them how hard you have worked for this opportunity. Acknowledge that others were also qualified, but it must have been your turn. Reinforce the possibility of other promotions coming up. Also talk about your changed role with them in a positive, friendly manner. Reinforce how much their friendship means to you. Emphasize that it's not you or them that has changed, it's the roles that have changed. Because of this role change, the relationships need to change also. Tell them that others in the department expect fairness and impartiality. As a supervisor you must provide this fair environment. Reinforce the idea that, as their manager, you will give them the support they need. In return, you need their cooperation and performance. You need to establish fair working relationships as you build trust and teamwork within your group.

Many people have trouble shifting to being a supervisor over their friends. If the honest, direct approach does not result in good working relationships then you may need additional help from a trusted, more experienced supervisor. Perhaps the beginning of a` mentor relationship can evolve from asking for help!

20

CONSTRUCTIVE DISCIPLINE

It's inevitable that you will be confronted with situations requiring disciplinary action. Some of the more common situations are excessive absenteeism, tardiness, inadequate work performance and poor attitudes which interfere with the work of others. A tendency most leaders have is to put off dealing with the situation. If you wait, some other employee will begin to bend the rules and "get away" with similar violations.

The purpose of disciplinary action is not to punish, but to improve the employee's future behavior. You should determine whether your organization has a policy and a set of procedures for disciplinary actions. If so, follow the procedures. If not, check with your superior for guidance.

Typical Disciplinary Actions Plan

Typically, disciplinary actions follow these general guidelines:

1. Employees should know in advance what is expected and what offenses lead to discipline.
2. Employees should know what the penalties are.
3. Discipline should be immediate. (If not, misperceptions occur.)
4. Discipline should be consistent. (Every violation is followed by some action.)

5. Discipline should be job related. (Don't get into personal accusations.)
6. Above all, your goal is to return the employee's behavior to acceptable performance levels.

In recent years, the trend has been to use positive discipline. This type of action stresses extensive coaching, counseling and problem-solving, and avoids confrontation. In general, this approach replaces warnings and suspensions with coaching sessions and reminders by the supervisor of the expected standards of performance.

Firing an Employee

Firing an employee is always a difficult decision. It also is one that the supervisor may not have the authority to make but can only recommend. This is primarily due to legal ramifications. Follow the procedures of your company.

Every effort should be made to develop, counsel and coach an employee to meet standards of performance; nevertheless, there will be some employees you will have to give up on.

21

MANAGING YOUR BOSS

You know you must manage subordinates. You know peer relationships need managing. But your boss is also critical. Get to know your boss's strengths, weaknesses, work style and needs. How does your boss prefer structuring meetings: formal agenda, pre-meeting reports or follow-up memos? Is your boss organized? Does s/he expect the same style from you or a complementary style? Is s/he the "big thinker" and you the follow-up "detail artist"? What goals, objectives and pressures does your boss have?

Nine Ways to Keep Relationships Effective

1. Don't be passive; talk it over with your boss. What would s/he prefer? Offer options or suggestions of how you can work together.
2. Keep your boss informed on current and anticipated problems and progress.
3. Keep communication open.
4. Don't hesitate to be firm when you need your boss's time and attention.
5. Do your homework; be prepared.
6. Be sensitive to the fact that your boss is ultimately responsible for your group's final results and understand why s/he's involved with your performance.
7. Be loyal and don't talk behind your boss's back; it'll eventually get back to her or him.

8. Don't forget your boss is human and enjoys the pleasant aspects of positive feedback—thank her/him for their support; if possible, a compliment in front of their superior is particularly appreciated.
9. Be sincere. Don't force it or get into the "pleasing others" trap.

22

MANAGING CONFLICT

What's Your Conflict Resolution Style?

It is inevitable that you will be called upon to resolve interpersonal conflicts. Interpersonal conflict involves two or more individuals who perceive themselves in opposition to each other regarding preferred outcomes.

We respond to interpersonal conflict in at least five different ways: avoiding, accommodating, compromising, forcing and collaborating. What's your style?

Five Conflict Resolution Styles—Pros and Cons

1. *The avoidance style* involves behavior that is unassertive and uncooperative. We use this style to stay out of conflicts, ignore disagreements or remain neutral. This approach is a decision to let the conflict work itself out, by itself. It is a subconscious aversion to tension and frustration. This is a passive style that, if used excessively, results in unfavorable reactions from others. Nevertheless, it can be useful if a conscious decision is made to use it and it is appropriate for the situation. An example of an appropriate use of avoidance is: Two subordinates have to vent frustration and talk through a problem that does not concern you or the company. Don't get involved, just listen.

2. **The forcing style** is assertive but uncooperative. It reflects a "win-lose" approach in that only one person or group wins. We use this when we have no concern for others and our desire to achieve our own goals is our primary concern. This approach involves elements of abused power and dominance. Forcing is not useful in long-term relationships—others will have unfavorable evaluations of you.
3. **The accommodating style** represents behavior that is cooperative but not assertive. This approach may be useful in a long-term action plan to encourage cooperation. It is a passive act. Its negative consequence? Being perceived as weak. It's useful if the group or individual you work with has much power (i.e. boss) and abuses their power *and* you.
4. **The compromising style** represents behavior that is between cooperative and assertive. It's a give and take process, and can involve negotiation and a series of concessions. Those who use it tend to be evaluated favorably. This style is commonly accepted by many. However, when compared to the collaborative style, it does not maximize joint outcomes.
5. **The collaborative style** is behavior that is strongly cooperative and assertive. It reflects a "win-win" approach. Both parties win. This style represents a desire to maximize joint outcomes. People who use this style see conflict as a natural process that leads to helpful, creative solutions. They see that a conflict resolution that satisfies all leads to commitment to the solution. They see others as equals having legitimate opinions. Others evaluate this style and the user favorably. A team approach in your management style accommodates this conflict solution style most of the time.

Each of us tends to utilize a particular style more frequently than others. The choice usually reflects a personality characteristic. Of course there are other factors that influence the choice such as attitude and the power of others, and the demands of the present situation.

What is your attitude toward conflict? Is it a positive or negative force in your organization? If you've answered negatively then you need to re-examine the process, purpose and end results of conflict. It can be a powerful force that aids problem-solving and decision-making. Conflict occurs when two or more parties are in opposition over their preferred outcomes. This actually describes a problem situation, doesn't it? There are many problems in groups, between individuals and departments. The benefits of conflict are many.

Six Benefits of Conflict

1. Conflict is a signal that a problem exists.
2. Through the constructive process of resolving conflict, we see trouble situations we weren't aware of.
3. We search for the means to change a problem.
4. The process of searching for ways to resolve conflict may lead to innovation and change.
5. Conflict may make necessary change more acceptable as well as point out the need for change.
6. Better decision-making and problem-solving occurs under conflict. Historians point to the governmental policy group that made Kennedy's Bay of Pigs Cuban crisis decision a prime example of making a decision without conflict. The policy group was very cohesive and desired agreement on a decision. They did not consider enough alternative solutions or the entire set of pros and cons before making their infamous decision. They didn't have conflict. No one wanted or could offer opposition to their decision because everyone agreed from the beginning. Decision-making is aided by conflict because more alternatives are generated and more complete evaluations are made of the problem situations.

However, conflict can also be a negative force if it's never resolved. A leader's attitude toward conflict determines whether it occurs openly and whether it's a positive force that invokes problem-solving behavior.

23

TEAM-BUILDING

How to Build a Team Approach

The effectiveness of your work group can be enhanced by systematically building a team orientation with your subordinates.

Six Team-Building Activities

1. Clarifying employee roles.
2. Building trust.
3. Inducing members to contribute to overall department performance.
4. Sharing the recognition of goal accomplishment.
5. Enhancing employee problem-solving skills.
6. Using participative management techniques.

Team-building is a process by which members of a work group diagnose how they work together and plan changes that improve their effectiveness. Team-building improves the effectiveness of work groups by having members focus on one or more of the following four purposes (Beckhard, 1972).

Four Areas Teams Can Work On

1. Setting goals and priorities for the group.
2. Analyzing and allocating the way work is performed.

3. Examining the way the group is working.
4. Examining relationships among the people doing the work.

How Teams Function

1. A team-building sequence begins when group members recognize a problem in the way they function together, set goals, allocate work or relate to each other.
2. Data is shared. Perceptions of issues, problems and working relationships are discussed.
3. The problem is analyzed and contributing factors are discovered. The real problems are diagnosed.
4. The group plans specific actions to resolve problems and assigns individuals to implement them. All participate in the plan.
5. At a later time, members share their evaluations of how the team is performing.

Team-building is an ongoing process which has many secondary benefits. In addition to creating a smooth-working team that accomplishes work unit goals, there are many benefits and advantages.

Advantages of Teams

1. A cooperative spirit is formed that accomplishes goals.
2. Subordinates become involved in a common goal.
3. A trusting atmosphere is created and employees feel they can function without threat.
4. Communication is open. Morale, listening and speaking skills are developed.
5. Subordinates learn decision-making and problem-solving skills.
6. Roles and job assignments are clarified.
7. Subordinates feel free to ask for assistance from each other.
8. Subordinates share responsibility.
9. Subordinates feel important, valued and challenged.
10. Cross-training can occur, which builds more generalists as opposed to specialists.
11. Leader intervention is needed less often because individuals have group assistance.
12. The leader is sending positive messages of recognition and trust.
13. Subordinates have room to function. This frees you to do more planning, organizing, controlling for results and individual subordinate diagnoses.
14. Mutual respect is fostered.
15. Future supervisors and managers are developed.

24

SOCIALIZING NEW EMPLOYEES

Informal Aspects of the Job and the Work Group

Many times we forget what we learned during those first weeks on a new job. The way a new employee is socialized into becoming a new team member determines that employee's success as well as the success of his/her contribution to the group effort. Just as a child is socialized to behave in appropriate ways and accept desired attitudes, a new employee must be socialized to act in a way and assimilate attitudes that the work team values.

Four Areas That Need Attention in the Socialization Process

1. Understanding how the team works.
2. Knowing that skills will be developed.
3. Learning cooperation, involvement, trust, open communication, freedom to ask for help, autonomy and respect for others.
4. Understanding the attitude that "we do things in a certain way; for example, we cooperate, not compete."

Orienting the New Employee

You will want to make this a pleasant experience. Don't overload the new employee with too much information at one time.

Formal Aspects of the Job

An effective orientation includes adequate attention to the possibility that this process will have a lasting effect. The first few days are disturbing and anxious for a new employee. An orientation should include: 1) a workplace explanation 2) an introduction to co-workers 3) a tour of the company 4) time to fill out the necessary employment papers 5) an explanation of the telephone system. Other information the new employee needs is: 1) starting and stopping times 2) proper work attire 3) parking facilities 4) lunch and break times 5) rate of pay 6) standards of performance 7) job evaluations and performance appraisals 8) how to report absences.

It is always desirable to assign a trusted employee to assist and accompany the new employee for the first week. Being supportive is a key concern.

Training and Development

New employees need training. How this is accomplished is dependent upon the training utilized in your organization. The most widely used method is called on-the-job training. The new employee is trained by a co-worker while actually performing the job. The supervisor may assist in the process. You should make periodic follow-up visits to see how the employee is doing.

Another training method is called off-the-job training where the employee is sent away for formal training while working part-time in the work unit.

When a team orientation exists in the work group, most of the training is done by the team. This enhances the training process and satisfaction of the team.

25

GIVING PERFORMANCE APPRAISALS

Performance appraisals are important to the employee, the supervisor and the organization. Appraising performance is part of the control process that is so important in keeping the efforts of people on track, accomplishing goals and objectives. Employees, supervisors and the organization have objectives. That's why the process is so important.

Six Steps to Effective Performance Appraisals

1. Provide feedback to the employee. This keeps the employee informed on where s/he stands. The strengths and weaknesses covered allow the employee to adjust efforts, direction and self-assessment.
2. Help the employee make career decisions. The assessment assists in mapping strategy to achieve career goals.
3. Help the organization make decisions regarding promotions, discipline, rewards, compensation and terminations.
4. Help the supervisor determine training and development needs. Leadership assists the employee in gaining skills and abilities to accomplish set goals, and readies the employee for advancement.
5. Provide guidance to the supervisor so s/he can give the necessary recognition, rewards or negative feedback.

6. Provide a vehicle to include the employee in the planning process. Participation in setting goals results in more effective implementation and accomplishment of goals.

Four Barriers to Giving Effective Appraisals

If performance appraisals have a bad reputation in an organization, it's because they haven't been done correctly.

1. Seeing the process as criticism. This is too narrow a view. Criticism and feedback are only part of the process.
2. Resisting giving performance appraisals because you've experienced them as a negative process. They should be viewed as a positive opportunity to interact with subordinates.
3. Not knowing how to give effective performance appraisals.
4. Employees may show resistance that causes you to resist the process. Prepare employees to accept performance appraisals as a positive part of learning.

Three Additional Advantages to Appraising

1. Encourages communication between the supervisor and subordinates.
2. Becomes a tool for planning and control, which are key management functions.
3. Helps the supervisor lead and coach employees.

Performance Appraisals Have a Cycle

The process is a constant repeating cycle. You and your subordinates set performance objectives. The appraisal gives feedback. Then the coaching aspect comes into play. After this, adjustment to appropriate objectives is done—you may need to change objectives. Again, the coaching function occurs to provide guidance. Then the appraisal. This process repeats itself all year long.

Six Steps to Giving Performance Appraisals

1. Set up a meeting in comfortable surroundings.
2. Review the employee's record.
3. Set an agenda of the meeting and give a copy to your subordinate.

4. Inform your employee to prepare for the meeting. Be sure they understand it's a mutual process. One good experience helps this attitude.
5. Discuss the issues on the agenda.
   a. Listen to your subordinate's self-assessment.
   b. Agree or disagree in a friendly tone.
   c. Summarize key points.
   d. Add your observations.
   e. Seek agreement between you and your subordinate.
   f. Track causes of any performance that is off track.
   g. Design a plan of action to remedy any deficiency.
   h. Reward on-track performance.
   i. Set goals for next year.
6. Throughout the year have two-way conversations that fit the cycle outlined above.

Three Areas to Focus On

1. Appraise the job-related behaviors, not anything else. Don't get into personalities, biases or attitudes.
2. Discuss the performance behavior of the employee. Positive and negative levels of performance need to be explained, including their effects on others' performance.
3. How the subordinate contributes to work group goal accomplishment needs to be outlined. This helps the subordinate's understanding of his/her importance to the team.

26

STRATEGY FOR IMPROVING YOUR PROMOTABILITY

Successful people have learned that they must concentrate on doing the best possible job in their current position while looking ahead to their next position.

Getting Into Supervisory Management

Ironically, the very qualities that make us outstanding performers in entry-level jobs are the ones that may hinder us from being effective supervisors. Also, after we become effective supervisors, we may find we must continually shift our attention to the requirements of the next level of management. Each level of management requires slightly different—as well as additional— skills, behaviors and efforts.

Let's look at some key characteristics of non-management workers.

Ten Characteristics of the Successful Entry-Level Worker

1. Hard working.
2. Technical expert.
3. Relies on self-performance.

4. Follows rules and procedures.
5. Performs relatively routine tasks.
6. Task-completion oriented.
7. Job-performance oriented.
8. Attends to details.
9. Has knowledge of the departmental requirements and goals.
10. Follows instructions of his/her supervisor.

Carole has these behaviors and characteristics. That's why she was promoted to supervisor. Carole continued to use these characteristics and found she wasn't effective as a supervisor. Why? She didn't understand that her new job required her to make sure her subordinates demonstrated those characteristics, not herself! Sure, she had to keep working hard. She had to know the technical aspects of the department, follow certain rules and procedures, know her department's goals and work with her boss. But she didn't seem to know that there was something else to supervising. If she isn't careful, the very characteristics and skills that got her promoted will get her demoted! She needs to shift out of the non-management orientation to become an effective supervisor. Let's look at some characteristics of successful supervisors.

Characteristics of Successful Supervisors

1. Carry out policies given to them from the level above.
2. Plan short-range action steps to carry out goals set by the level above.
3. Organize the work group.
4. Assign jobs to subordinates.
5. Delegate projects to subordinates.
6. Direct tasks, jobs and projects.
7. Train subordinates.
8. Enforce rules.
9. Lead and motivate subordinates.
10. Develop group cohesiveness.
11. Solve routine daily problems.
12. Control or evaluate performance of subordinates and the department—performance appraisals.
13. Discipline subordinates.
14. "Doing" can be up to 70 percent of the time—(this varies according to the type of supervisory job—the doing involves the actual work of the department as well as the planning, controlling, scheduling, organizing, leading, etc.).

Carole must shift to planning, scheduling, assigning, delegating, organizing, training, leading, solving problems, developing group spirit, tracking subordinates and department performance. In short, Carole must change from:

1. Follower to leader.
2. Reactor to planner.
3. Specialist to generalist.
4. "Doer" to delegator.
5. Follower of rules to enforcer of rules.

Advancing to Middle-Level Management

We face the same dilemma as when we entered supervisory management. What do we need to know to get promoted and how can we be effective? The strategy to advancing beyond the supervisory level involves a clear idea of where you want to go.

Strategic Steps to Advancing

1. Know and learn the skills and methods of middle management.
2. Your career plan needs mapping step by step. Chart your course. Set goals. Start a visibility campaign and demonstrate your promotability.
3. Get a mentor.
4. Get to know your company from top to bottom. Know how it works inside and out. Investigating and researching this impresses superiors. This knowledge is needed by middle managers.

Know and Learn the Skills and Methods of Middle Management

1. The skills of planning, controlling, organizing and leading are still required, but the emphasis is changed from short term to long term; from routine to non-routine; from grouping tasks to grouping people into departments; from specific details to broader generalities; from enforcing policies to making policies; from observing performance to checking progress via reports; from managing down to managing up, down and laterally; from reliance on positional authority to reliance on interpersonal persuasion; from physically supervising to monitoring reports...and a multitude of other differences.
2. Some new skills have to be learned such as coordinating multiple departments' efforts, negotiating for cooperation between groups, resolving inter-departmental conflict, analyzing complex, non-

routine problems and making decisions that affect more people.
3. Methods of middle management involve a greater use of the political networking of reciprocal obligations. Middle managers must rely on bases of power and influence other than positional authority because many times they actually have no authority over the people they must work with (i.e. other departments, managers on the same level, level-up bosses). Credibility becomes a prime concern and behavior, track record and image become the only sources of influence. Doing occupies 30-40 percent of the time and delegating 60-70 percent. The "doing" part of the job involves the planning, controlling, organizing, leading, coordinating, negotiating, resolution of conflicts, solution of complex problems and also routine work like paperwork, writing reports and analyzing information.

A Career Plan Needs Mapping Step by Step

1. Where do you want to be in 10 years? What do you want to be doing? What is feasible and would fulfill you?
2. Where do you need to be in five years? How are you going to get there? What positions do you need to get to in four, three and two years? What is the next position you will get promoted to?
3. Select your next position. Start getting ready for it. If you need qualifications such as a degree, a course, more accounting or leadership training, go get it!
4. You've got your goals for promotion set. Now start your strategy of getting the visibility to improve your promotability. A visibility campaign involves selling yourself. Take on projects with high visibility. Get on a task group that has powerful people on it. Be seen before the day begins and after the day ends. Ask questions, be interested in the total organization. Show initiative. Demonstrate high performance.

Get a Mentor

1. Your personal path to advancement can be littered with boulders. We all have strengths and weaknesses. We need help to recognize and overcome the weaknesses and build on strengths. Don't think you're the only one who doesn't know everything. All people need help. It's being able to ask for it that separates the effective from the ineffective.

Don't ever assume that you are the only one with insecurities and doubts. I've interviewed hundreds of successful businesswomen and the vast majority have reluctantly shared a deep secret. The secret being they thought a magic final sense of confidence would occur when they achieved a long sought-after goal such as a hard-fought promotion, recognition or acceptance by the "Old Boy" network. It didn't occur and they still fought the battle daily: "How am I perceived?" "Am I saying and doing the right thing?" "Did I wear the right clothes?" "Was my voice clear?" "Was that a dumb idea I proposed?" "Will I be discounted?" In summary, no man or woman manager arrives at a destination; it's a continuous process of trying.

To traverse this path, you need to seek a person to guide your career development. Your mentor can be another supervisor, a company executive, an associate, a spouse, a friend or a professor. Your mentor can help open doors for you and help you make the important decisions. A mentor can assist you to see your current job as only one of a series in your career; help you learn your job; assist you in game-playing, political techniques and image-building; help you recognize your weaknesses; instruct you in learning about your company and its industry; assist you in personal goal-setting and help you gain visibility with those who can help.

Ultimately a mentor chooses you, but you can gain their attention with a demonstrated desire to advance. Let it be known you want a career at performance appraisal time, etc. Tactfully ask for feedback on projects. Ask for assignments and do an excellent job. Above all, be professional and rely on your expertise and competence.

Use professional groups in your community. There are many professional women's groups to become involved in. These informal contacts can help you learn about everything from dressing for success to technical advice on a statistical problem. These groups are full of women who want to help. Also, don't forget community service projects where you'll meet men and women, have fun and learn a lot about management. In fact, many corporations encourage community service because it is a training ground for developing and practicing management skills with volunteers! It's a "win-win" situation for you. You can practice and not feel threatened about job security!

Get to Know Your Company

1. Get your company's organizational chart. Learn the parts and how they fit together. Know the names of the people in key

positions. Look at people who are advancing; study and learn
from them. Be visible. Learn what each department does and how
it coordinates with other departments. Find out what your company's long-range strategy is. What are its major goals? Know the
nature of the industry. What are the major goals? How does a
company compete? Demonstrate you have the "big-picture"
orientation.

Give Yourself Permission to Throw Away "Old Tapes"

1. *Take risks.* Nothing ventured, nothing gained.
2. *Accept and give criticism.* You can't learn without feedback on
   what needs changing.
3. *You can't be perfect.* Perfection can be an excuse for not trying.
4. *You can't please everyone.* Sometimes there are more rewards in
   pleasing yourself by doing a good job.
5. *Don't trade being respected for being liked.* You may find you
   get both in the process.
6. *Indirectness pleases no one.* How will others know what you
   want or expect if you don't say it?

The Choice is Yours!
Good Luck and Good Managing

INDEX

Notes

Notes

Notes

Notes

Buy two, get one free!

Each of our handbook series (LIFESTYLE, COMMUNICATION, PRODUCTIVITY and LEADERSHIP) was designed to give you the most comprehensive collection of hands-on desktop references all related to a specific topic. They're a great value at the regular price of $12.95 ($14.95 in Canada); plus, at the unbeatable offer of buy two at the regular price and get one free, you can't find a better value in learning resources. **To order**, see the back of this page for the entire handbook selection.

1. Fill out and send the entire page by mail to:

National Press Publications
6901 West 63rd Street
P.O. Box 2949
Shawnee Mission, Kansas 66201-1349

2. Or **FAX 1-913-432-0824**

3. Or call toll-free **1-800-258-7248**

Fill out completely:

Name _____
Organization _____
Address _____
City _____
State/Province _____ ZIP/Postal Code _____
Telephone ( ) _____

Method of Payment:
☐ Enclosed is my check or money order
☐ Please charge to:
   ☐ MasterCard   ☐ Visa   ☐ American Express

Signature _____ Exp. Date _____
Credit Card Number

☐☐☐☐☐☐☐☐☐☐☐☐☐☐☐☐

To order multiple copies for co-workers and friends:	U.S.	Can.
20-50 copies	$8.50	$10.95
More than 50 copies	$7.50	$ 9.95

VIP# 705-00463-092

OTHER DESKTOP HANDBOOKS

	Qty.	Item #	Title	U.S.	Can.	Total
LEADERSHIP		410	The Supervisor's Handbook, Revised and Expanded	$12.95	$14.95	
		458	Positive Performance Management: *A Guide to Win-Win Reviews*	$12.95	$14.95	
		459	Techniques of Successful Delegation	$12.95	$14.95	
		463	Powerful Leadership Skills for Women	$12.95	$14.95	
		494	Team-Building	$12.95	$14.95	
		495	How to Manage Conflict	$12.95	$14.95	
		469	Peak Performance	$12.95	$14.95	
		418	Total Quality Management	$12.95	$14.95	
COMMUNICATION		413	Dynamic Communication Skills for Women	$12.95	$14.95	
		414	The Write Stuff: *A Style Manual for Effective Business Writing*	$12.95	$14.95	
		417	Listen Up: *Hear What's Really Being Said*	$12.95	$14.95	
		442	Assertiveness: *Get What You Want Without Being Pushy*	$12.95	$14.95	
		460	Techniques to Improve Your Writing Skills	$12.95	$14.95	
		461	Powerful Presentation Skills	$12.95	$14.95	
		482	Techniques of Effective Telephone Communication	$12.95	$14.95	
		485	Personal Negotiating Skills	$12.95	$14.95	
		488	Customer Service: *The Key to Winning Lifetime Customers*	$12.95	$14.95	
		498	How to Manage Your Boss	$12.95	$14.95	
PRODUCTIVITY		411	Getting Things Done: *An Achiever's Guide to Time Management*	$12.95	$14.95	
		443	A New Attitude	$12.95	$14.95	
		468	Understanding the Bottom Line: *Finance for the Non-Financial Manager*	$12.95	$14.95	
		489	Doing Business Over the Phone: *Telemarketing for the '90s*	$12.95	$14.95	
		496	Motivation & Goal-Setting: *The Keys to Achieving Success*	$12.95	$14.95	
LIFESTYLE		415	Balancing Career & Family: *Overcoming the Superwoman Syndrome*	$12.95	$14.95	
		416	Real Men Don't Vacuum	$12.95	$14.95	
		464	Self-Esteem: *The Power to Be Your Best*	$12.95	$14.95	
		484	The Stress Management Handbook	$12.95	$14.95	
		486	Parenting: *Ward & June Don't Live Here Anymore*	$12.95	$14.95	
		487	How to Get the Job You Want	$12.95	$14.95	

SALES TAX All purchases subject to state and local sales tax. Questions? Call **1-800-258-7248.**		
	Subtotal	
	Sales Tax (Add appropriate state and local tax)	
	Shipping & Handling ($1 one item, 50¢ each add.)	
	Total	

VIP# 705-00463-092